More
Favorite Traditional Quilts
Made Easy

JO PARROTT

Martingale®
& COMPANY

More Favorite Traditional Quilts Made Easy
© 2010 by Jo Parrott

That Patchwork Place® is an imprint
of Martingale & Company®.

Martingale & Company
20205 144th Ave. NE
Woodinville, WA 98072-8478 USA
www.martingale-pub.com

Printed in China
15 14 13 12 11 10   8 7 6 5 4 3 2 1

Library of Congress Cataloging-in-Publication Data is available upon request.

ISBN: 978-1-56477-979-3

Mission Statement

Dedicated to providing quality products
and service to inspire creativity.

Credits

President & CEO: Tom Wierzbicki
Editor in Chief: Mary V. Green
Managing Editor: Tina Cook
Developmental Editor: Karen Costello Soltys
Technical Editor: Nancy Mahoney
Copy Editor: Marcy Heffernan
Design Director: Stan Green
Production Manager: Regina Girard
Illustrator: Laurel Strand
Cover & Text Designer: Adrienne Smitke
Photographer: Brent Kane

Dedication

To my family, every one of them, beginning with my husband Henry and all of our children, grandchildren, and great-grandchildren.

Contents

Introduction

What's the first thing you see when you look at a quilt? Color, of course. If you're lucky enough to have a good eye for color, your quilts will show it. If you don't, find someone you trust who can help you with fabric and color selections. But be aware, if you rely on someone else, you may end up making a quilt that they like more than you do.

Color is such an individual thing. I encourage you to make your own fabric choices to create that one-of-a-kind quilt. After selecting your fabrics, the process of how you make the quilt becomes front and center, so to speak. We have a lot of choices today that our grandmothers didn't.

My first quilt, in 1982, was hand pieced and hand quilted. My second quilt was machine pieced using strips that had been cut with a new gadget called a rotary cutter. Back then, self-healing mats and acrylic rulers didn't have lines; acrylic rulers came in various widths instead of the array of precision-marked rotary-cutting rulers that we have today. As you can imagine, it wasn't easy to tell at a glance whether you were cutting 2"- or 2½"-wide strips! Even so, rotary cutters sped up the cutting process. But time-saving gadgets and machines also created some debate as to whether quilts made using these shortcuts were *really* handmade quilts.

In the late 1980s, machine quilting with a home sewing machine came along. Many quilters refused to do this—I know because I was one of them! Then one day I saw a hand-quilted quilt I had given a grandchild just 6 months earlier. It looked like it was 20 years old. It was then that I realized there is a place for both hand and machine quilting. I want my grandchildren to love and use the quilts I give them, and it doesn't matter to them how the quilt was made. Since then, machine quilting has certainly sped up my ability to make quilts.

When our grandchildren began giving us great-grandchildren and I started writing books, I couldn't produce quilts fast enough. Now I use a long-arm quilting machine. Modern tools and techniques have allowed me to quilt 101 quilts in the last 28 months.

I feel we should use the tools we have available to us. They make it easier to make the quilts we love—even quilts that years ago seemed to be for only the most skilled quiltmakers. Enjoy what you make and keep on quilting!

Quiltmaking Tips

As we visit and meet with quilting friends, we hear tips and ideas. You may have heard some of the following, maybe not. They are, however, tips that I do use. I hope you find one that will help you.

CUTTING TIPS

- To me the most essential tool is a *sharp* rotary cutter. Replacement blades for rotary cutters come packaged slightly oily. This excess oil is part of the manufacturing process and should be wiped off, but don't wipe the blade clean. A little oil will help keep your blade rolling smoothly in your cutter. To extend the life of the blade, after some use, open your cutter and clean the blade removing any lint. Then place a small drop of sewing machine oil on the blade and spread it around on both sides to lubricate the blade.

- Once you've got a rotary cutter, you need a clear, acrylic ruler and self-healing cutting mat. I find always using the same ruler makes cutting easier, simply because you become so familiar with its lines and markings that mistakes happen less frequently.

- A comfortable table height is critical when doing a lot of cutting. If you get a backache when cutting, your table is probably too low, and you need to raise it—an inch or two can make a big difference. Place a brick or block of wood under each table leg to raise your table to a comfortable height. Just make sure the bricks or wood blocks are all the same size.

- When cutting strips into squares or rectangles, don't move the fabric after cutting the strips. If you need to turn the strips, turn the whole mat.

- Organize as you cut. Save small, flat cardboard boxes or box lids. Stack your cut pieces in the box and, if needed, make notes on the cardboard about the sizes of the pieces.

- Label your rotary cutter, mat, rulers, and other tools before heading off to a class or retreat. Many quilters have the same tools and gadgets, and you want to be able to identify yours.

SEWING AND PRESSING TIPS

- When drawing a line on fabric, hold the pencil like you'd hold a cake knife, at a low angle with your index finger on top to guide it. Drawing this way keeps the pencil sharp and helps prevent the fabric from moving.

- The best investment I've made for quilting is a single-hole throat plate for my sewing machine. The small needle hole prevents the fabric from being punched down into the bobbin, allowing you to start a nice clean seam. (Just be sure to change it before using the zigzag or blanket stitch!)

- If you don't have thread that matches the fabric, use gray. It blends nicely with most colors.

- Use a sharp seam ripper with a large handle that will fit in the palm of your hand.

- After removing stitches with a seam ripper, use an emery board to find and remove the little pieces of thread.

- Cut the tails of threads as you go. It's so much easier than saving them all for the end of your project. And if you leave them attached, they may show through on your finished quilt.

- A comfortable chair is a necessity for sewing. Invest in a good chair—it's worth the cost.

- Sew an accurate ¼" seam allowance. To check your accuracy, cut seven fabric strips, each exactly, 1½" x 6½". Sew six strips together along their long edges. Press the seam allowances to one side. Sew the last strip to the top of the rectangle; it should be an exact fit. The resulting square should measure 6½" x 6½".

- Assembly-line (or chain) sewing is fast and accurate. Do it whenever possible. It also helps you keep track of the pieces you've sewn. For instance, if you need to make 100 units, sew them in smaller batches of 25. Repeat four times and you're done!

- Many times when sewing, it's necessary to pin pieces together. Pins are usually placed perpendicular to the seam you'll be sewing. I find that occasionally it's useful to place pins parallel to the seam line; this helps keep the seam allowances on the bottom piece from catching on the feed dogs and getting turned in the wrong direction. Just make sure the tip of the pin is pointing toward the sewing machine and remove each pin as it reaches the presser foot. This way the pieces are held in place longer, and the newly sewn seam isn't distorted as you remove the pin.

- Many quilters have a pressing area within reach of where they sew; then they don't even have to move. I have my ironing board across the room, so I have to stand up and move around. It's good to move!

- When pressing half-square-triangle units, place the piece that the seam allowance is to be pressed toward on the top. Lift the corner of the top fabric and use the tip of the iron to gently push the fabric over the seam allowance. Leave the unit on the ironing board; press the next unit, overlapping the units slightly. Repeat 8–10 times, and then move the stack. Pressing goes so much faster this way.

MISCELLANEOUS TIPS

- Pace yourself. Whether cutting or sewing, you'll do a better job if you aren't too tired.

- Make yourself take a break or do a chore, like dusting, vacuuming, or baking cookies to break up long stints of quilting.

- Keep notepads everywhere and make notes. You never know when you'll see a quilt design or hear a quilting tip you want to remember.

- When you see a pattern you might want to make but aren't quite sure, make it smaller, such as a lap quilt or table runner. You'll know before you finish the small item if you want to make a larger quilt. Plus, you'll use up some scraps and make a gift in the process.

- If you want to know how much time you really spend on a quilt, set an electric clock, one with hands, at 12:00. Plug it in when you start a project, unplug it when you stop, plug it back in when you go back to working on the quilt. When you reach 12:00 again, make a note of the hours and continue until the project is made. Check the clock and your notes to see how many hours are there. Keep in mind, a digital clock won't work as it resets to 12:00 each time it's plugged in.

- I use the extra fabric trimmed from the backing to make a sleeve for a quilt as soon as I finish the binding. It gets done quickly and matches the backing fabric.

- To protect yourself, in case of theft, write your name, address, and phone number inside the sleeve or on the quilt back behind the sleeve with a permanent pen.

- Save scraps in plastic tubs, by color. This makes putting fabrics together for a scrap quilt so much easier. I can store 16 large tubs under my long-arm quilting-machine table, making good use of the space.

- If you are concerned about the colors in your fabrics running, use a dye grabber in the washer the first time you launder the quilt. If some excess dye bleeds and causes staining, wash again with a bleach-for-colors product.

- Last tip—make time for what *you* want to do.

A Storm at Sea

Pieced and quilted by Jo Parrott, 2008

The Storm at Sea quilt design has been around for years. To be honest, I'd never even seen a Storm at Sea quilt in person, just in pictures. It's a quilt that I'd always wanted to make but never did because of the long, thin triangles. Now, because we can use rectangles, I expect to see many of these quilts.

Finished quilt: 85½" x 109½"
Finished block: 12" x 12"

FABRIC SELECTION

Fabric requirements are given as fabrics 1–5, which are also used throughout the instructions. This will make it easier for you to choose your own color scheme and still get the fabrics in the right places in the quilt layout. I recommend taping swatches of each fabric to a numbered 3" x 5" card so you can see at a glance which fabric goes with which number.

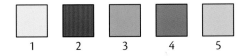

MATERIALS

Yardage is based on 42"-wide fabric.
2⅝ yards of fabric 1 (pale blue) for blocks
7½ yards of fabric 2 (dark blue) for blocks, outer border, and binding
2⅓ yards of fabric 3 (medium blue) for blocks
1 yard of fabric 4 (medium dark blue) for blocks
4⅜ yards of fabric 5 (bright teal) for blocks and inner border
8¼ yards of fabric for backing fabric*
91" x 115" piece of batting

If using 108"-wide fabric, you'll need 3½ yards.

CUTTING

Cut all strips across the width of fabric (selvage to selvage).

From fabric 1, cut:
8 strips, 6½" x 42"; crosscut into 96 rectangles, 3" x 6½"
5 strips, 3¾" x 42"; crosscut into 48 squares, 3¾" x 3¾". Cut squares in half diagonally to yield 96 triangles.
6 strips, 2⅜" x 42"; crosscut into 96 squares, 2⅜" x 2⅜". Cut squares in half diagonally to yield 192 triangles.

From fabric 2, cut:
12 strips, 8½" x 42"; crosscut into 96 rectangles, 4½" x 8½"
10 border strips, 5½" x 42"
3 strips, 4⅞" x 42"; crosscut into 24 squares, 4⅞" x 4⅞". Cut squares in half diagonally to yield 48 triangles.
6 strips, 4½" x 42"; crosscut into 48 squares, 4½" x 4½"
6 strips, 2⅞" x 42"; crosscut into 72 squares, 2⅞" x 2⅞". Cut squares in half diagonally to yield 144 triangles.
10 binding strips, 2¼" x 42"

From fabric 3, cut:
8 strips, 6½" x 42"; crosscut into 96 rectangles, 3" x 6½"
3 strips, 4⅞" x 42"; crosscut into 24 squares, 4⅞" x 4⅞". Cut squares in half diagonally to yield 48 triangles.
3 strips, 2½" x 42"; crosscut into 48 squares, 2½" x 2½"

From fabric 4, cut:
6 strips, 4⅞" x 42"; crosscut into 48 squares, 4⅞" x 4⅞". Cut squares in half diagonally to yield 96 triangles.

From fabric 5, cut:

15 strips, 6½" x 42"; crosscut into 192 rectangles, 3" x 6½"

5 strips, 3¾" x 42"; crosscut into 48 squares, 3¾" x 3¾". Cut squares in half diagonally to yield 96 triangles.

2 strips, 2⅞" x 42"; crosscut into 24 squares, 2⅞" x 2⅞". Cut squares in half diagonally to yield 48 triangles.

9 border strips, 2" x 42"

UNIT ASSEMBLY

Each block is made up of four units; a large and a small square-in-a-square unit, a pieced rectangle, and a mirror-image pieced rectangle.

Unit 1

1. With the square on top, sew 2⅜" fabric 1 triangles to opposite sides of a 2½" fabric 3 square as shown, making sure the dog-ears of fabric 1 are sticking out equally on each side of the square. Turn the unit right side facing up and press the seam allowances toward the triangles.

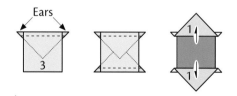

2. In the same manner, sew matching triangles to the remaining sides of the square. Press and trim off the dog-ears.

3. Repeat step 1 to sew a 2⅞" fabric 5 triangle to one side and a 2⅞" fabric 2 triangle to the opposite side of the unit from step 2. Press the seam allowances toward the triangles.

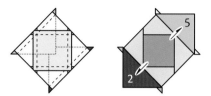

4. Sew 2⅞" fabric 2 triangles to the remaining two sides of the unit. Press and measure; the unit should measure 4½" x 4½". If it doesn't, adjust your seam allowances. Repeat to make a total of 48 identical units.

Unit 1.
Make 48.

Adjusting Seam Allowances

If the unit measurement is larger than 4½" x 4½", your seam allowances are too narrow and should be slightly wider. If the unit measurement is smaller than 4½" x 4½", your seam allowances are too wide and should be slightly narrower. Keep in mind that it may take only a small adjustment to your seam allowance to achieve a 4½" x 4½" unit. It's better to sew an accurate seam allowance than to rely on "squaring up" the completed unit. Make sure you have a full ¼" seam allowance beyond the outside points, otherwise corners will be cut off when the block is assembled.

Unit 2

Unit 2 is made in the same manner as unit 1; however, the pieces are larger so unit 2 measure 8½" x 8½".

1. Sew a 3¾" fabric 1 triangle to one side of a 4½" fabric 2 square. Sew a 3¾" fabric 5 triangle to the opposite side of the square. Press the seam allowances toward the triangles.

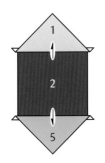

2. In the same manner, sew triangles to the remaining sides of the square as shown. Press and trim off the dog-ears.

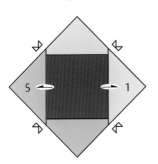

3. Sew a 4⅞" fabric 2 triangle to the fabric 1 side of the unit from step 2. Sew a 4⅞" fabric 3 triangle to the opposite side of unit as shown. Press the seam allowances toward the triangles.

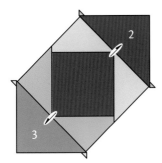

4. In the same manner, sew 4⅞" fabric 4 triangles to each remaining side of the unit. Press and trim off the dog-ears. Make a total of 48 identical units. Each unit should be 8½" x 8½".

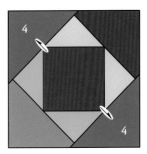

Unit 2.
Make 48.

Unit 3

Unit 3 is a 4½" x 8½" rectangle; you'll also need to make a mirror image of unit 3 for each block. It's easiest to make all unit 3s first, and then make the mirror-image units. That way, you'll be less likely to get a fabric in the wrong position.

1. For accurate sewing, mark the *wrong* side of a 4½" x 8½" fabric 2 rectangle with dots. All dots should be placed *exactly* midway along each side of the rectangle and ¼" from the raw edge. So, mark the dots on the short ends of the rectangle 2¼" from the corners, and the dots on the long sides of the rectangle 4¼" from the corners. Draw lines connecting the dots to precisely mark the sewing lines.

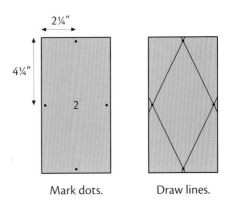

Mark dots.   Draw lines.

2. With the *wrong* side of the marked rectangle facing up so you can see the drawn lines, position a 3" x 6½" fabric 1 rectangle right side facing up underneath the marked rectangle with at least ¼" of fabric extending beyond the marked line as shown. Sew on the drawn line.

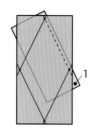

3. In the same manner, sew a 3" x 6½" fabric 3 rectangle to the opposite corner of the unit from step 2. Press the seam allowances toward the outside corners.

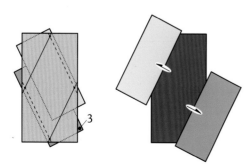

4. Place the unit right side facing down on a cutting mat. Use your rotary cutter to trim fabrics 1 and 3 even with the fabric 2 rectangle as shown.

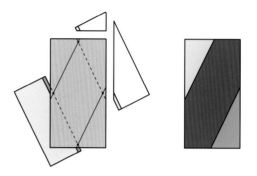

5. Repeat steps 3 and 4 to sew, press, and trim 3" x 6½" fabric 5 rectangles to the two remaining corners of the unit. Repeat to make a total of 48 units, each measuring 4½" x 8½". (I leave the bottom layer [fabric 2] intact, because it helps stabilize the corners and keep the piece square; however, you can trim away the excess in the corners, leaving a ¼"-wide seam allowance, if you don't want two thicknesses of fabric.)

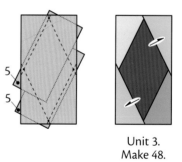

Unit 3.
Make 48.

6. Repeat steps 1–5 to make 48 mirror-image units. Begin at the corner shown using a 3" x 6½" fabric 1 rectangle.

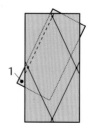

Unit 3 reversed.
Make 48.

BLOCK ASSEMBLY

1. Lay out one of each unit, making sure to position unit 3 and mirror-image unit 3 as shown. Sew the units together to make a total of 48 blocks.

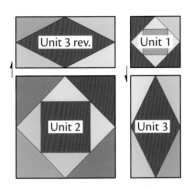

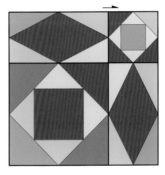

Make 48.

2. Arrange and sew the blocks in groups of four, making sure to position each block so that unit 1 is oriented in the center of the larger unit. Make 12 four-block units.

Make 12.

QUILT TOP ASSEMBLY

1. Lay out the four-block units in four rows of three blocks each. Sew the blocks together in rows. Press the seam allowances in opposite directions from one row to the next. Then sew the rows together and press the seam allowances in one direction.

Quilt layout

2. Referring to "Adding Borders" on page 42 and using the 2"-wide strips of fabric 5 for the inner border and the 5½"-wide strips of fabric 2 for the outer border, add the borders to your quilt.

FINISHING THE QUILT

Layer the quilt with batting and the pieced backing; baste. Hand or machine quilt with the quilting design of your choice. Refer to "Binding Your Quilt" on page 43 and use the 2¼"-wide fabric 2 strips to bind your quilt.

COLOR OPTION: A STORM AT SEA

PIECED AND QUILTED BY JO PARROTT, 2008

MATERIALS AND CUTTING

Refer to the materials and cutting lists on page 9 and use the red color swatches below for easy reference.

1   2   3   4   5

ASSEMBLY

Using the block layout diagram below, assemble the blocks as described on pages 10–13.

Broken Star

Pieced and quilted by Jo Parrott, 2008

The Broken Star design is sometimes called The Star of Bethlehem. It's a beautiful quilt, but because of all the diamonds, many quilters don't attempt it. I have developed a method of labeling the fabrics, and then strip piecing that makes it much easier.

Finished quilt: 102½" x 102½"

FABRIC SELECTION

Fabric requirements are given as fabrics 1–7, starting with fabric 1 in the center of the star. These numbers are also used throughout the instructions. This will make it easier for you to choose your own color scheme and still get the fabrics in the right places in the quilt layout. I recommend taping swatches of each fabric to a numbered 3" x 5" card so you can see at a glance which fabric goes with which number.

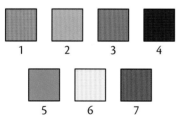

MATERIALS

Yardage is based on 42"-wide fabric.
½ yard of fabric 1 for diamonds
¾ yard of fabric 2 for diamonds
1⅛ yards of fabric 3 for diamonds
1⅜ yards of fabric 4 for diamonds
1⅛ yards of fabric 5 for diamonds
¾ yard of fabric 6 for diamonds
½ yard of fabric 7 for diamonds
4¼ yards of light print for background
3¼ yards of dark print for border and binding
9½ yards of fabric for backing
108" x 108" piece of batting

CUTTING

Cut all strips across the width of fabric (selvage to selvage).

From *each* fabric for diamonds, cut the number of 2¾" x 42" strips indicated:
Fabric 1; cut 4 strips
Fabric 2; cut 8 strips
Fabric 3; cut 12 strips
Fabric 4; cut 16 strips
Fabric 5; cut 12 strips
Fabric 6; cut 8 strips
Fabric 7; cut 4 strips

From the light print for background, cut:
9 border strips, 1½" x 42"

From the dark print for border and binding, cut:
11 border strips, 6½" x 42"
11 binding strips, 2¼" x 42"

DIAMOND UNITS

The diamonds are made from four different strip-set units. After sewing each seam, press the seam allowances toward the lowest fabric number.
1. Using the 2¾"-wide strips, arrange the strips in groups of four as shown. Stagger the strips by about 2½" and sew fabric 1 and 2 strips together along their long edges to make a strip pair. Stagger the strips; sew fabric 3 and 4 strips together to make a second strip pair. Then, staggering the strip pairs, sew them together

to complete strip-set unit 1, as shown. In the same manner, sew the appropriate strips together to make each unit as indicated. Make four of each unit.

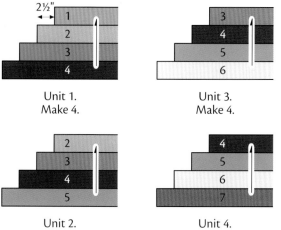

Unit 1.
Make 4.

Unit 3.
Make 4.

Unit 2.
Make 4.

Unit 4.
Make 4.

2. Using the 45° line on your cutting mat, lay unit 1 on the mat with the staggered ends extending beyond the 45° line. Place the long edge of the unit along any horizontal line as shown. Using a ruler and rotary cutter, place the ruler on the 45° line and trim off the irregular end of the strip-set unit. *Do not* move the unit at this time. Measure 2¾" from the freshly cut end of the strip and cut a 2¾"-wide segment. Repeat cutting two or three 2¾"-wide segments. Stack the segments together.

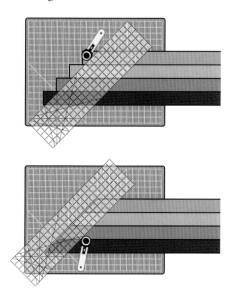

3. After cutting two or three segments, move the strip-set unit over to the 45° line, aligning the long edge along a horizontal line on the mat, as before. Make sure the cut end is even with the 45° line. If not, trim as needed. Cut two or three 2¾"-wide segments. Continue in this manner, cutting a total of 32 segments from the unit 1 strip sets. Set the remaining strip set aside to make the "Bonus Project" on page 22.

4. Repeat steps 2 and 3, cutting 2¾"-wide segments from all of the strip-set units. Cut a total of 32 segments *each* from units 2, 3, and 4. Stack all matching segments together.

DIAMOND ASSEMBLY

To make accurate diamond units that don't bow or become distorted, careful pressing is essential. Move the tip of your iron between the sewn segments. Then turn the iron to the side so the long edge of the iron gently presses the top segment over the seam allowance. It's important that the diamond units stay straight and don't become distorted.

1. To make one diamond unit, lay out one segment from each unit as shown. Place two segments right sides together and pin to match seam intersections. The ends of the segments will be offset ¼" as shown. Sew the segments together using a ¼"-wide seam allowance. Pin and sew the remaining two segments together in the same manner.

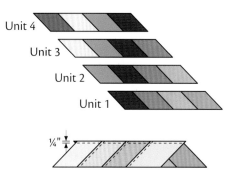

Unit 4

Unit 3

Unit 2

Unit 1

¼"

Positioning Pins

A positioning pin will help you match two points. On the wrong side of the top segment, stick a straight pin through the seam allowance, ¼" from the edge of the segment. (This is where the stitching line will cross the existing seam.) Separate the two segments so you can see to insert the pin through the second segment. Insert the pin through the second segment, ¼" from the raw edge, and pierce the seam. Keep the pin upright and loose. Repeat for each seam intersection. With the positioning pins still in place, place a straight pin on either side of each positioning pin to hold the matching points in place. Pin all seam intersections, allowing a ¼" tip to overlap both ends. Remove the positioning pins before stitching.

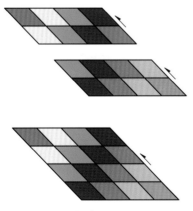

2. Press the seam allowances in one direction; the ends should be straight along the outside edge as shown. Sew the two pairs together to make a pieced diamond. Make a total of 32 diamonds.

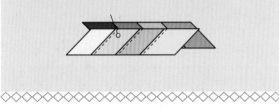

Make 32.

3. On the wrong side of a diamond unit, align the ¼" mark on a ruler with the raw edge in one corner. Use a pencil to lightly mark ¼" from the edge in preparation for Y-seam construction. Mark the tips and corners of each diamond unit.

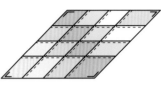

Mark corners.

CENTER STAR ASSEMBLY

You'll use eight of the diamond units to make the center star.

1. Pin two diamond units right sides together, matching the seam intersections. Starting at the diamond tip, sew the seam, and then stop at the ¼" mark with a backstitch. Make a total of four diamond pairs. Carefully press the seam allowances to one side.

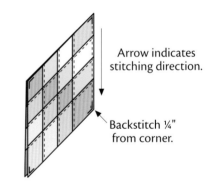

Arrow indicates stitching direction.

Backstitch ¼" from corner.

2. Sew two diamond pairs together in the same manner to make a half-star unit; pressing the seam allowances to one side. Repeat to make a second half-star unit.

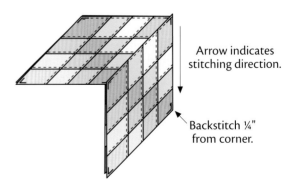

Arrow indicates stitching direction.

Backstitch ¼" from corner.

3. With right sides together, align and pin the two half-star units together, matching the seam intersections. Sew the center seam, starting and stopping at the ¼" marks with a backstitch. Press the seam allowances to one side.

4. Once the star is assembled, you'll have two types of grain line along the outer edges of the diamond units; one side is bias and the other side is straight grain. Therefore, you'll need to measure all 16 sides of the diamond units to get an average measurement. Measure each side between the ¼" marks. Write the measurement on a piece of paper and estimate the average. If your measurements range from 12½" to 13"; the average measurement would be 12¾". Using the remaining background fabric, cut 12 squares, four rectangles, and eight quarter-square triangles, referring to "Cutting the Setting Pieces" at right.

5. In the same manner as the diamond units, mark the corners of each setting piece ¼" from the edge in preparation for Y-seam construction.

CUTTING THE SETTING PIECES

Before cutting the squares, rectangles, and triangles from the background fabric for the setting pieces, you'll need to add a seam allowance to each piece. For example, if the average measurement of the diamond units is 12¾", you'd need setting pieces in the sizes indicated.

For the squares, add ½" seam allowances (12¾" + ½" = 13¼"). Cut 12 squares, 13¼" x 13¼".

For the rectangles, the short side is the same as the cut square size (13¼"). For the long side, multiply 12¾" by 2 and add ½" to the result for seam allowances (12¾" x 2 = 25½" + ½" = 26"). Cut 4 rectangles, 13¼" x 26".

For the triangles, multiply 12¾" by 1.414 and add 1¼" to the result for seam allowances (12¾" x 1.414 = 18" + 1¼" = 19¼"). Cut 2 squares, 19¼" x 19¼". Fold each square in half vertically and then horizontally, as shown, to make a 9⅝" square. Cut each folded square in half diagonally, as shown to yield 4 quarter-square triangles (8 total).

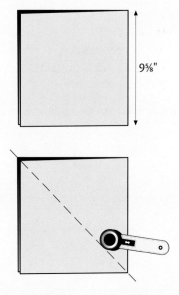

9⅝"

6. Place a background square on top of a diamond unit, right sides together. Align the raw edges, matching the ¼" mark on the background square to the ¼" mark on the diamond unit beneath it. Sew from the outside edge to the inside corner, starting and stopping at the ¼" marks with a backstitch. Press the seam allowances toward the square.

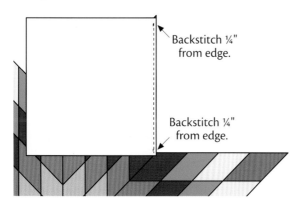

7. With right sides together, position the second diamond unit on top of the square. Align the raw edges and match the ¼" marks. Sew from the outside edge to the inside corner, starting and stopping at the ¼" marks with a backstitch. Press the seam allowances toward the square.

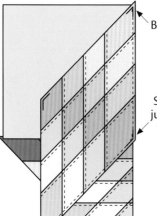

8. Repeat steps 6 and 7, sewing background squares to the inner corners as shown to complete the center star section.

QUILT TOP ASSEMBLY

1. In the same manner as step 1 in "Center Star Assembly," sew three diamond units together. Start at the diamond tip and stop at the ¼" mark with a backstitch. Make a total of eight 3-diamond units. Carefully press the seam allowances to one side.

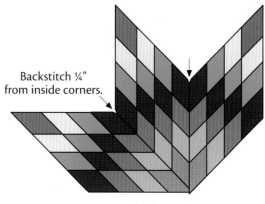

Make 8 units.

2. In the same manner as step 7 in "Center Star Assembly" sew a 3-diamond unit to a background square. Sew from the outside edge to the inside corner, starting and stopping at the

¼" marks with a backstitch. *Do not* sew past the ¼" marks.

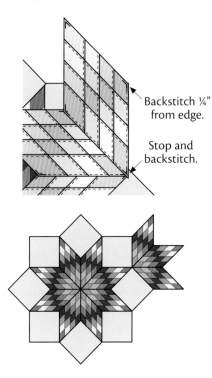

Backstitch ¼" from edge.

Stop and backstitch.

3. Continue around the center star, adding 3-diamond units to the background squares, and then stitching the seam between adjoining units. Be sure to always start and stop at the ¼" marks with a backstitch.

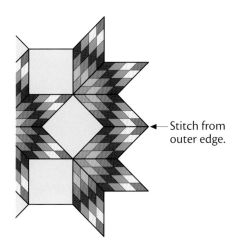

Stitch from outer edge.

4. Arrange the eight background quarter-square triangles around the unit from step 3 as shown. In the same manner as steps 6 and 7 in "Center Star Assembly," sew the triangles in place, starting at the outside edge

and stopping at the ¼" marks with a backstitch. Press the seam allowances toward the triangle.

5. Sew the four remaining background squares to the diamond units, starting at the outside edge and stopping at the ¼" marks with a backstitch. Then sew the four background rectangles to the unit.

6. Referring to "Adding Borders" on page 42 as needed and using the 1½"-wide background strips for the inner border and the 6½"-wide dark strips for the outer border, add the borders to your quilt.

FINISHING THE QUILT

Layer the quilt with batting and the pieced backing; baste. Hand or machine quilt with the quilting design of your choice. Refer to "Binding Your Quilt" on page 43 and use the 2¼"-wide dark strips to bind your quilt.

Bonus Project

Every once in a while you get an added bonus to a quilt. This is one of those times. If you accurately cut all of diamond-unit segments when making the "Broken Star" quilt on page 15, you'll have enough leftovers to make this wall hanging.

PIECED AND QUILTED BY JO PARROTT, 2008

Finished quilt: 59" x 59"

ADDITIONAL MATERIALS

1⅜ yards of a light print for background and inner border
½ yard of green fabric for middle border
1⅛ yards of floral for outer border
⅝ yard fabric for binding

CUTTING

From the light print, cut:
5 border strips, 1½" x 42"
4 squares, 13¼" x 13¼"*
1 square, 19¼" x 19¼"; cut diagonally into quarters to make 4 side setting triangles*

*You may want to wait until the star is assembled to measure and cut the corner squares and side setting triangles. Refer to "Cutting the Setting Pieces" on page 19, before cutting these pieces.

From the green fabric, cut:
5 border strips, 2" x 42"

From the floral, cut:
6 border strips, 5½" x 42"

From the binding fabric, cut:
7 binding strips, 2¼" x 42"

QUILT TOP ASSEMBLY

Cut 8 more 2¾"-wide segments from each remaining strip-set unit to make eight diamond units for the star points, referring to "Diamond Assembly" on page 17 as needed. Assemble the star and add the background squares and triangles as described on pages 18–20. (Note that triangles replace the squares on the sides of the star.) Use the 1½"-wide background strips for an inner border to make the star float away from the darker borders. Use the 2"-wide green strips for the middle border and the 5½"-wide floral strips for an outer border. Quilt as desired, and use the 2¼"-wide floral strips for binding.

Geese in Flight

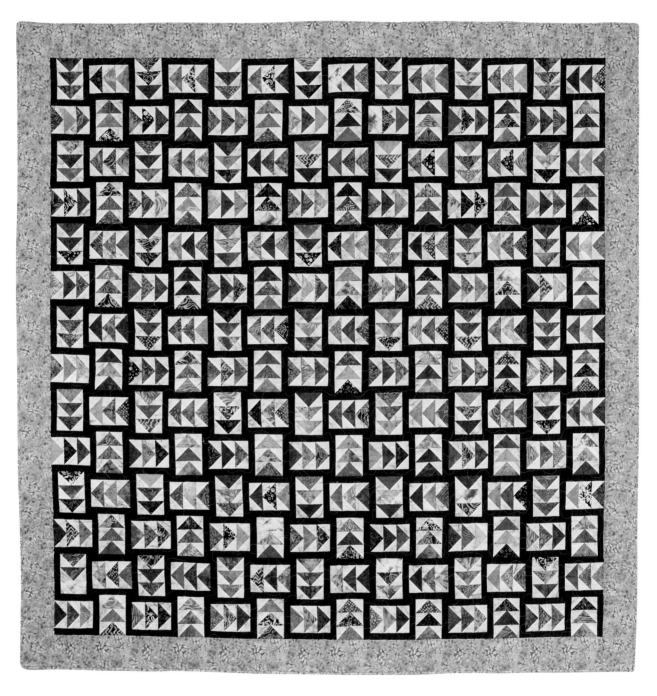

Pieced and quilted by Jo Parrott, 2008

The Geese in Flight quilt can be made from a variety of fabric scraps or just batik scraps, like I used. If you like one-color scrap quilts, you can use strips from your blue stash, green stash, or whatever color you choose. Each 4½" x 42" strip will make 16 "geese."

Finished quilt: 96½" x 96½"
Finished block: 12" x 12"

MATERIALS

Yardage is based on 42"-wide fabric.
5¾ yards of a light fabric for block backgrounds
5 yards *total* of assorted scraps and/or batik
　　fabrics for blocks
3¼ yards of a dark print for sashing
2⅞ yards of fabric for border and binding
9¼ yards of fabric for backing*
102" x 102" batting

*If using 108"-wide fabric, you'll need 3 yards.

CUTTING

Cut all strips across the width of fabric (selvage to selvage). When using scraps, the strips can be cut crosswise or lengthwise to get the longest cut.

From the light fabric for block background, cut:
74 strips, 2½" x 42"; crosscut into 1176 squares, 2½" x 2½"

From the assorted scraps and/or batik fabrics, cut a total of:
37 strips, 4½" x 42"; crosscut into 588 rectangles, 2½" x 4½"

From the dark print for sashing, cut:
16 strips, 6½" x 42"; crosscut into 392 rectangles, 1½" x 6½"

From the fabric for border and binding, cut:
10 border strips, 6½" x 42"
10 binding strips, 2¼" x 42"

BLOCK ASSEMBLY

Directions are for one block. Each block is assembled using 12 different scrap/batik 2½" x 4½" rectangles and 24 background 2½" squares. Repeat to make a total of 49 blocks.

1. Draw a diagonal line from corner to corner on the wrong side of the background squares. Place a marked square on one end of a scrap/batik rectangle, right sides together and raw edges aligned. Sew on the marked line and trim away the corner fabric, leaving a ¼"-wide seam allowance. Press the resulting triangle open.

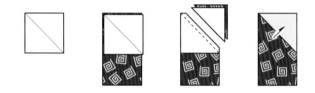

2. Place a marked background square on the opposite end of the rectangle, positioning the square as shown. Sew, trim, and press in the same manner. Repeat to make a total of 12 flying-geese units.

Make 12.

3. Sew three flying-geese units together as shown. Press the seam allowances in one direction. Repeat to make a total of four units.

Make 4.

Bonus Half-Square Triangles

If you want to make use of the extra corner fabric, stitch a second seam ½" from the first seam as shown. Cut between the two stitching lines. You'll have the rectangle and triangle unit, plus a half-square triangle for another project.

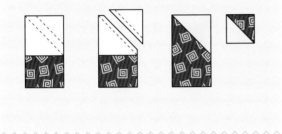

4. Sew 1½" x 6½" dark rectangles to opposite sides of each unit from step 3. Press the seam allowances toward the rectangles.

Make 4.

5. Lay out the units in a four-patch arrangement as shown. Sew the units together in rows, and then sew the rows together to complete a block. Press all seam allowances toward the sashing strips. Make a total of 49 blocks.

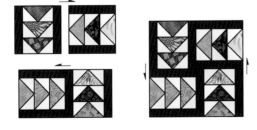

QUILT TOP ASSEMBLY

1. Lay out the blocks in seven rows of seven blocks each. Rearrange the blocks as desired until you are pleased with the arrangement.
2. Sew the blocks together into rows, pressing the seam allowances in opposite directions from one row to the next. Then sew the rows together and press the seam allowances in one direction.

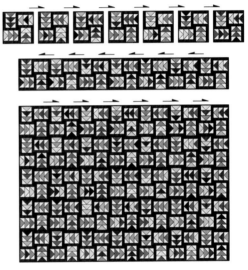

Quilt layout

3. Referring to "Adding Borders" on page 42 and using the 6½"-wide outer-border strips, add the borders to your quilt.

FINISHING THE QUILT

Layer the quilt with batting and the pieced backing; baste. Hand or machine quilt with the quilting design of your choice. Refer to "Binding Your Quilt" on page 43 and use the 2¼"-wide strips to bind your quilt.

Stars on the Water

PIECED AND QUILTED BY JO PARROTT, 2008

The name for this quilt came about after a class I taught. Someone asked me what my quilt was called, and I replied I really hadn't named it. One of the students, Linda, said it reminded her of stars on the water. So after that, anytime I said something about the quilt, I called it the "Stars on the Water" quilt. I think that must be the way a lot of patterns are named.

Finished quilt: 69½" x 81½"
Finished block: 9" x 9"

MATERIALS

Yardage is based on 42"-wide fabric.

3¼ yards light floral for block backgrounds, sashing, and inner border

3 yards of green fabric for sashing star points, outer border, and binding

2⅛ yards of dark purple fabric for block star points

1⅛ yards of light lavender fabric for four-patch units

1⅛ yards of dark lavender fabric for four-patch units

5¼ yards of fabric for backing*

75" x 87" piece of batting

*If using 90"-wide fabric, you'll need 2¼ yards.

CUTTING

Cut all strips across the width of fabric (selvage to selvage).

From the light lavender fabric, cut:
17 strips, 2" x 42"

From the dark lavender fabric, cut:
17 strips, 2" x 42"

From the light floral, cut:
21 strips, 3½" x 42"; crosscut into 231 squares, 3½" x 3½"
2 strips, 6½" x 42"; crosscut into 18 rectangles, 3½" x 6½"
7 border strips, 2½" x 42"

From the dark purple fabric, cut:
15 strips, 4½" x 42"; crosscut into 240 rectangles, 2¼" x 4½"

From the green fabric, cut:
18 strips, 4½" x 42"; crosscut *10 of the strips* into 160 rectangles, 2¼" x 4½" (Set aside the remaining strips for the outer border.)
8 binding strips, 2¼" x 42"

BLOCK ASSEMBLY

1. With right sides together, join 2"-wide light lavender strips and dark lavender strips along their long edges using a ¼"-wide seam allowance. Press the seam allowances toward the darker strip. Repeat to make a total of 17 strips sets. From the strip sets, cut 340 segments, 2" wide.

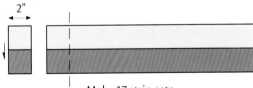

2"

Make 17 strip sets.
Cut 340 segments.

2. Sew the segments from step 1 together in pairs to make 170 four-patch units. (Assembly-line sewing makes the sewing go faster.) Press the seam allowances to one side. Set 20 four-patch units aside to use for the quilt assembly.

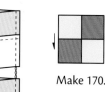

Make 170.

3. For accurate sewing, mark the wrong side of a 3½" light floral square with dots. The first dot should be placed *exactly* midway along one side of the square and ¼" from the raw edge, as shown. Mark the opposite corners, ⅛" from the edge, as shown. Mark 120 squares in this manner.

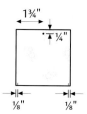

4. Draw lines connecting the dots to mark the sewing lines.

Draw lines.

5. With the *wrong* side of the marked square facing up so you can see the drawn lines, position a 2¼" x 4½" dark purple rectangle *right* side facing up underneath the square with at least ¼" of fabric extending beyond the marked line as shown. Sew on the drawn line. Press the purple rectangle open.

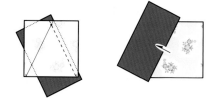

6. In the same manner, sew a second purple rectangle to the unit from step 5 and press. Place the unit right side facing down on a cutting mat. Use your rotary cutter to trim the purple rectangles even with the background square. You can leave the bottom layer of light floral intact to help stabilize the corners and keep the piece square, or, you can trim away the excess fabric (leaving a ¼"-wide seam allowance) if you don't want

two layers of fabric. Make 120 star-point units.

Make 120.

7. Lay out the five four-patch units and four star-point units in a nine-patch arrangement, making sure to arrange them as shown so that the dark lavender squares are all going in the same direction. Sew the units together into rows, pressing the seam allowances toward the four-patch units, and then sewing the rows together. Press. Repeat to make a total of 30 blocks.

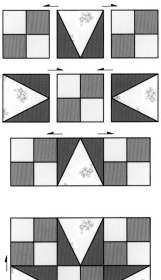

Make 30.

SASHING STRIP ASSEMBLY

1. Repeat steps 3–6 in "Block Assembly" using 80 of the 3½" light floral squares and the 2¼" x 4½" green rectangles. Make a total of 80 green star-point units.

2. Sew a 3½" light floral square between two green star-point units as shown and press. Make a total of 31 sashing units.

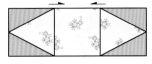

Make 31.

3. Sew a green star-point unit to one end of each 3½" x 6½" light floral rectangle as shown and press. Make a total of 18 end units.

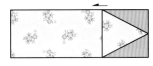

Make 18.

QUILT TOP ASSEMBLY

1. Lay out the blocks, sashing units, and end units in rows, making sure to arrange the blocks as shown below so that the dark lavender squares are all going in the same direction. There are three different row configurations.

2. Sew the blocks and units together in rows, pressing the seam allowances toward the blocks or four-patch units. Make the number of rows indicated for each arrangement.

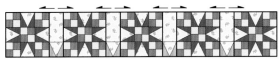

Top/bottom row.
Make 2.

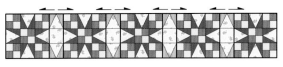

Make 4.

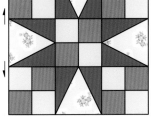

Sashing row.
Make 5.

3. Arrange and sew the rows together as shown in the layout diagram. Press the seam allowances toward the sashing rows.

4. Referring to "Adding Borders" on page 42 as needed and using the 2½"-wide light floral strips for the inner border and the 4½"-wide green strips for the outer border, add the borders to your quilt.

FINISHING THE QUILT

Layer the quilt with batting and the pieced backing; baste. Hand or machine quilt with the quilting design of your choice. Refer to "Binding Your Quilt" on page 43 and use the 2¼"-wide green strips to bind your quilt.

Quilt layout

Floral Table Runner

I always try to keep some extra items around that I have made to give as gifts when the occasion arises. This table runner has become a favorite. The beautiful fabrics just add to the design.

Finished table runner: 17" x 85"
Finished block: 12" x 12"

MATERIALS

Yardage is based on 42"-wide fabric.
1 yard of light floral for block backgrounds and setting triangles
⅝ yard of dark purple fabric for block star points
⅜ yard of dark green fabric for four-patch units
⅜ yard of light green fabric for four-patch units
1⅜ yards of fabric backing

CUTTING

Cut all strips across the width of fabric (selvage to selvage).

From the dark green fabric, cut:
4 strips, 2½" x 42"

From the light green fabric, cut:
4 strips, 2½" x 42"

From the light floral, cut:
3 strips, 4½" x 42"; crosscut into 20 squares, 4½" x 4½"
2 squares, 18¼" x 18¼"; cut diagonally into quarters to yield 8 setting triangles

From the dark purple fabric, cut:
3 strips, 5¾" x 42"; crosscut into 40 rectangles, 2¾" x 5¾"

From the backing fabric, cut:
2 pieces, 20" x 45" from the *lengthwise* grain

MADE BY JO PARROTT, 2009

BLOCK ASSEMBLY

These blocks are constructed in the same manner as the blocks in "Stars on the Water" (page 26), except the blocks are larger. For detailed instructions and illustrations on the following techniques, refer to "Block Assembly" on page 27.

1. With right sides together, join 2½"-wide light green strips and dark green strips along their long edges and press the seam allowances toward the darker strip. Repeat to make a total of 4 strips sets. From the strip sets, cut 50 segments, 2½" wide.

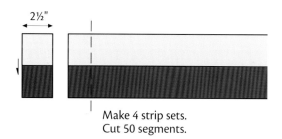

2½"

Make 4 strip sets.
Cut 50 segments.

2. Sew the segments from step 1 together in pairs to make 25 four-patch units. Press the seam allowances to one side.

3. Mark the wrong side of each 4½" light floral square with dots. The first dot should be placed *exactly* midway, or 2¼", along one side of the square and ¼" from the raw edge. Mark the opposite corners, ⅛" from the edge. Draw lines connecting the dots to mark the sewing lines.

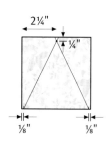

2¼"

¼"

⅛"   ⅛"

4. With the *wrong* side of the marked square facing up so you can see the drawn lines, position a purple rectangle right side facing up underneath the square with at least ¼" of fabric extending beyond the marked line. Sew on the drawn line and press the purple rectangle open.

5. In the same manner, sew a second purple rectangle to the unit from step 4 and press. Place the unit right side facing down on a cutting mat. Use your rotary cutter to trim the purple rectangles even with the background square. You can leave the bottom layer of light floral intact or you can trim away the excess fabric, leaving a ¼"-wide seam allowance. Make 20 star-point units.

6. Lay out five four-patch units and four star-point units in a nine-patch arrangement, making sure to arrange them as shown so that the dark green squares are all going in the same direction. Sew the units together into rows, pressing the seam allowances toward the four-patch units, and then sew the rows together; press. Repeat to make a total of 5 blocks.

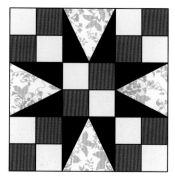

Make 5.

TABLE RUNNER ASSEMBLY AND FINISHING

1. Arrange the blocks and the light floral triangles together in diagonal rows, making sure the dark green squares are positioned as shown so that they run the length of the table runner. Sew the blocks and triangles into rows. Press the seam allowances toward the triangles.

2. Sew the rows together and press.

3. Sew the two pieces of backing fabric together, end to end, and press the seam allowances open. Center the table runner on top of the backing, right sides together, and pin in place. Using a ¼"-wide seam allowance, stitch all the way around the outer edge, leaving a 6" opening on one side for turning. Note that there is no batting in this table runner; however, if desired, you can use a thin filler, such as prewashed flannel.

Leave open.

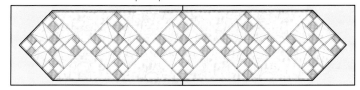

4. Trim the excess backing even with the table runner and turn it right side out through the opening. Pin the opening closed and topstitch around the outer edge, ⅛" from the edge. Stitch around blocks and along the seam lines to hold the layers together.

Pieced and quilted by Jo Parrott, 2009

A great novelty print is so much fun to use. The green frogs on the pink background just called to me, but any novelty print that calls your name would work. Enjoy!

Finished quilt: 59½" x 59½"
Finished block: 12" x 12"

Materials

Yardage is based on 42"–wide fabric.

- 1⅞ yards of small pink print for blocks and outer border
- 1⅞ yards of bright green fabric for blocks and binding
- 1¾ yards of focus fabric for blocks
- 1⅜ yards of blue fabric for blocks and inner border
- ⅜ yard of dark green fabric for blocks
- 4 yards of fabric for backing
- 65" x 65" piece of batting

Cutting

Cut all strips across the width of fabric (selvage to selvage).

From the small pink print, cut:

- 3 strips, 6½" x 42"; crosscut into 32 rectangles, 3" x 6½"
- 1 strip, 4⅞" x 42"; crosscut into 8 squares, 4⅞" x 4⅞". Cut squares in half diagonally to yield 16 triangles.
- 6 border strips, 4½" x 42"
- 1 strip, 2½" x 42"; crosscut into 16 squares, 2½" x 2½"

From the blue fabric, cut:

- 3 strips, 6½" x 42"; crosscut into 32 rectangles, 3" x 6½"
- 2 strips, 3¾" x 42"; crosscut into 16 squares, 3¾" x 3¾". Cut squares in half diagonally to yield 32 triangles.
- 2 strips, 2⅜" x 42"; crosscut into 32 squares, 2⅜" x 2⅜". Cut squares in half diagonally to yield 64 triangles.
- 5 border strips, 2" x 42"

From the bright green fabric, cut:

- 5 strips, 6½" x 42"; crosscut into 64 rectangles, 3" x 6½"
- 2 strips, 3¾" x 42"; crosscut into 16 squares, 3¾" x 3¾". Cut squares in half diagonally to yield 32 triangles.
- 1 strip, 2⅞" x 42"; crosscut into 8 squares, 2⅞" x 2⅞". Cut squares in half diagonally to yield 16 triangles.
- 6 binding strips, 2¼" x 42"

From the focus fabric, cut:

- 4 strips, 8½" x 42"; crosscut into 32 rectangles, 4½" x 8½"
- 1 strip, 4⅞" x 42"; crosscut into 8 squares, 4⅞" x 4⅞". Cut squares in half diagonally to yield 16 triangles.
- 2 strips, 4½" x 42"; crosscut into 16 squares, 4½" x 4½"
- 2 strips, 2⅞" x 42"; crosscut into 24 squares, 2⅞" x 2⅞". Cut squares in half diagonally to yield 48 triangles.

From the dark green fabric, cut:

- 2 strips, 4⅞" x 42"; crosscut into 16 squares, 4⅞" x 4⅞". Cut squares in half diagonally to yield 32 triangles.

These blocks are constructed in the same manner as the blocks in "A Storm at Sea" (page 8). For detailed instructions and illustrations on the following techniques, refer to "Block Assembly" on page 38.

Each block is made up of four units; a large and a small square-in-a-square unit, a pieced rectangle, and a pieced mirror-image rectangle.

Unit 1

1. With the square on top, sew 2⅜" blue triangles to opposite sides of a 2½" pink square as shown, making sure the dog-ears of blue fabric are sticking out equally on each end of the square. Turn the unit right side facing up and press the seam allowances toward the triangles.

2. In the same manner, sew matching triangles to the remaining sides of the square. Press and trim off the dog-ears.

3. Repeat step 1 to sew a 2⅞" bright green triangle to one side and a 2⅞" focus fabric triangle to the opposite side of the unit from step 2. Press the seam allowances toward the triangles.

4. Sew 2⅞" focus fabric triangles to the remaining two sides of the unit. Press and measure; the unit should measure 4½" x 4½". Repeat to make a total of 16 identical units.

Unit 1.
Make 16.

Unit 2

Unit 2 is made in the same manner as unit 1; however, the pieces are larger, so unit 2 measure 8½" x 8½".

1. Sew a 3¾" blue triangle to one side of a 4½" focus fabric square. Sew a 3¾" bright green triangle to the opposite side of the square. Press the seam allowances toward the triangles. In the same manner, sew a 3¾" blue triangle and a 3¾" bright green triangle to the remaining sides of the square as shown. Press and trim off the dog-ears.

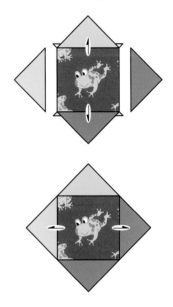

2. Sew a 4⅞" focus fabric triangle to the blue side of the unit from step 1. Sew a 4⅞" pink print triangle to the opposite side of unit as shown. Press the seam allowances toward the triangles.

3. In the same manner, sew 4⅞" dark green triangles to each remaining side of the unit. Press and trim off the dog-ears. Make a total of 16 identical units, measuring 8½" x 8½".

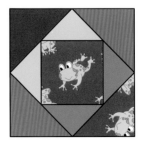

Unit 2.
Make 16.

Unit 3

Unit 3 is a 4½" x 8½" rectangle; you'll need to make a mirror image of unit 3 for each block. It's easiest to make all unit 3s first; then make the mirror-image units. That way, you'll be less likely to get a fabric in the wrong position.

1. Mark the wrong side of each 4½" x 8½" focus fabric rectangle with dots. All dots should be placed *exactly* midway along each side of the rectangle and ¼" from the raw edge. So, mark the dots on the short ends of the rectangle 2¼" from the corners, and the dots on the long sides of the rectangle 4¼" from the corners. Draw lines connecting the dots to mark the sewing lines.

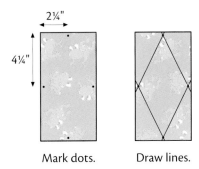

Mark dots.   Draw lines.

2. With the *wrong* side of the marked rectangle facing up so you can see the drawn lines, position a 3" x 6½" blue rectangle *right* side facing up underneath the rectangle with at least ¼" of fabric extending beyond the marked line as shown. Sew on the drawn line. In the same manner, sew a 3" x 6½" pink print rectangle on the opposite corner of the unit. Press the seam allowances toward the outside corners.

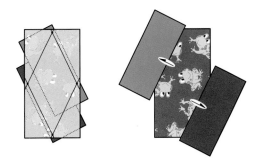

3. Place the unit right side facing down on a cutting mat. Use your rotary cutter to trim the blue fabric and pink print even with the focus fabric rectangle. The unit should be 4½" x 8½".

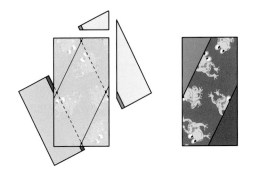

4. Repeat steps 2 and 3 to sew, press, and trim 3" x 6½" bright green rectangles to the two remaining corners of the unit. Repeat to make a total of 16 units, each measuring 4½" x 8½". You can leave the bottom layer (focus fabric) intact to help stabilize the corners and keep the piece square, or you can trim away the excess in the corners, leaving ¼" seam allowance.

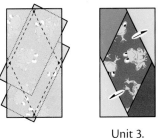

Unit 3.
Make 16.

5. Repeat steps 1–4 to make 16 mirror-image units. Begin at the corner shown using a 3" x 6½" blue rectangle.

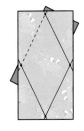

Unit 3 reversed.
Make 16.

BLOCK ASSEMBLY

1. Lay out one of each unit, making sure to position unit 3 and mirror-image unit 3 as shown. Sew the units together to make a total of 16 blocks.

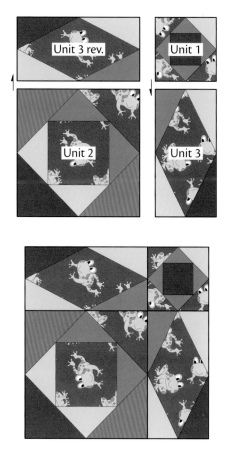

Make 16.

2. Referring to the layout diagram, arrange and sew the blocks in groups of four, making sure to position each block so that unit 1 is oriented to the center of the larger unit. Make 4 four-block units.

QUILT TOP ASSEMBLY

1. Lay out the four-block units in two rows of two blocks each. Sew the blocks together in rows. Press the seam allowances in opposite directions from one row to the next. Then sew the rows together and press the seam allowances in one direction.

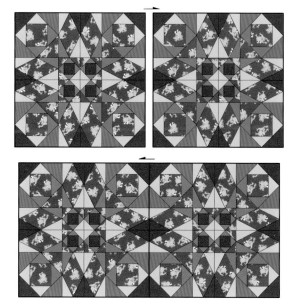

Quilt layout

2. Referring to "Adding Borders" on page 42 and using the 2"-wide blue strips for the inner border and the 4½"-wide pink print strips for the outer border, add the borders to your quilt.

FINISHING THE QUILT

Layer the quilt with batting and the pieced backing; baste. Hand or machine quilt with the quilting design of your choice. Refer to "Binding Your Quilt" on page 43 and use the 2¼"-wide bright green strips to bind your quilt.

Scrappy Rectangles

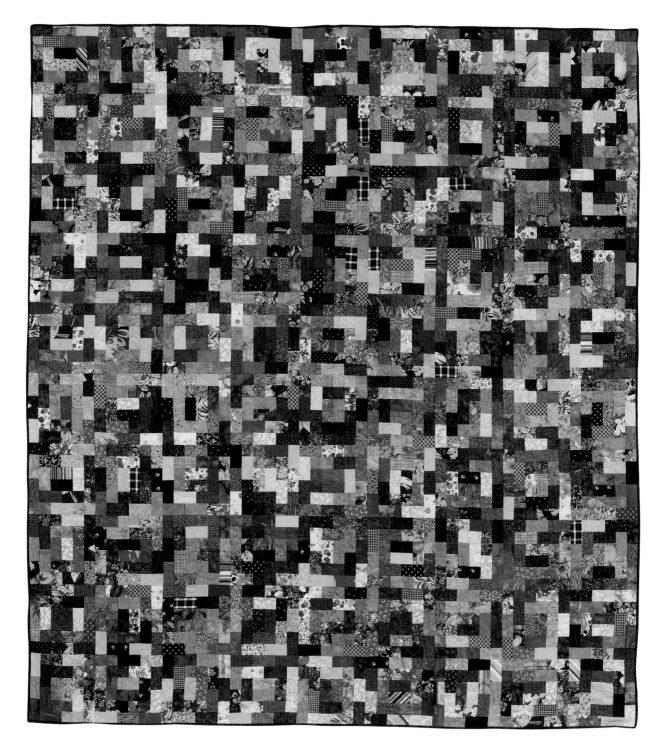

Pieced and quilted by Jo Parrott, 2008

*I often call this quilt 2" x 3½"
Scrappy Quilt for the size of each piece
used. It can and should be made from
scraps. However, one version I made
to be auctioned off for cancer research
started with half-yard pieces of 18
different fabrics. Since there are 18
rectangles in each block, I used a
different fabric for each rectangle.
Then I randomly stitched the blocks
together to get the scrappy effect. And
I still had enough fabric left over
from the half-yard pieces to make
another quilt.*

Finished quilt: 81½" x 90½"
Finished block: 9" x 9"

FABRIC SELECTION

You can tackle the fabric selection and cutting in
a number of ways. I keep a box by the table when
I cut out a quilt and immediately cut the
2" x 3½" rectangles from scraps as I go, so that
I'll have them for a quilt such as this one. I've
made several of these quilts, and on one occasion
I pulled tubs of scrap fabrics one color at a time
to cut pieces.

If you don't have tubs of scraps, use the
scraps you have and add some fat quarters. If you
want to purchase fat quarters, you'll need 36 fat
quarters to make all of the blocks.

As you cut, just put all the 2" x 3½" rectangles in the same box and don't pay attention
to which pieces you're sewing together. It's a fun
quilt to make, so enjoy!

MATERIALS

Yardage is based on 42"–wide fabric.
8⅝ yards *total* of assorted scraps for blocks
⅔ yard of fabric for binding
8 yards of fabric for backing*
87" x 96" piece of batting

*If using 108"-wide fabric, you'll need 2⅞ yards.

CUTTING

From the assorted scraps, cut a total of:
1620 rectangles, 2" x 3½"

From the binding fabric, cut:
9 strips, 2¼" x 42"

BLOCK ASSEMBLY

Directions are for making one block. Repeat
to make a total of 90 blocks. You may want to
assembly-line sew the blocks in groups, making
four or five blocks at a time. After sewing each
seam, press the seam allowances in the direction
indicated by the arrows.

1. Sew two rectangles together along their long
   sides. Sew a rectangle to the top and bottom.

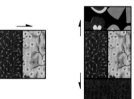

2. Sew two rectangles together end to end.
   Make two and sew them to the sides of the
   unit from step 1.

3. Sew two rectangles together end to end. Make two and sew them to the top and bottom of the unit from step 2.

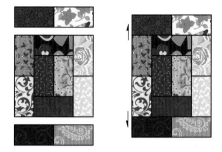

4. Sew three rectangles together end to end. Make two and sew them to the sides of the unit from step 3. Make a total of 90 blocks.

Make 90.

QUILT TOP ASSEMBLY

1. Arrange the blocks in 10 rows of nine blocks each, rotating every other block 90° as shown in the layout diagram.
2. Sew the blocks into rows. Press the seam allowances in opposite directions from one row to the next. Then sew the rows together and press the seam allowances in one direction.

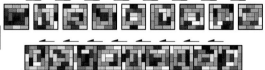

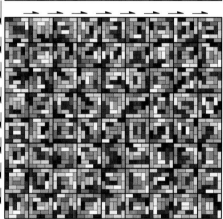

Quilt layout

3. Baste around the quilt top ⅛" from the outer edge to stabilize the seams, being careful not to stretch the seams as you sew.

FINISHING THE QUILT

Layer the quilt with batting and the pieced backing; baste. Hand or machine quilt with the quilting design of your choice. Refer to "Binding Your Quilt" on page 43 and use the 2¼"-wide fabric strips to bind your quilt.

Finishing Touches

Once the blocks are completed, you'll need to decide if you want to add borders. Then you can finish the quilt, which includes piecing the backing, layering and basting the layers, quilting the quilt, applying the binding, making a sleeve, and finally adding a label. The following instructions will help you with adding borders, binding, and a sleeve to your quilt.

ADDING BORDERS

The projects in this book provide examples of borderless quilts and quilts with simple borders. Sometimes an inner border is added from the same fabric as the background. This *floats* the blocks as in the "Broken Star" quilt on page 15. A beautifully pieced top can become an off-centered, uneven quilt if the borders are not added correctly. The main objective is to keep the quilt square so that it hangs straight and lies flat.

The quilts in this book that include borders call for plain border strips. The strips are cut crosswise selvage to selvage and joined end to end with a diagonal or straight seam where extra length is needed. There is a slight give in the fabric when the strips are cut in this manner, but it takes less fabric than when you cut strips from the lengthwise grain (parallel to the selvage).

I have not given any measurements for cutting your border-strip lengths. These measurements are determined once your quilt top is put together, as described in the border method that follows.

1. Measure the length of the quilt in three places. If the measurements are not all the same, average them. For example, if the three measurements are 88½", 88¾", and 89", the average would be 88¾". Cut two strips the length determined for the side borders, piecing as necessary.

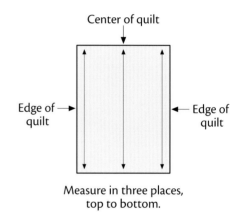

Measure in three places,
top to bottom.

2. Mark the center of the quilt edges and border strips. Pin the borders to the sides of the quilt top, matching the centers and ends. Ease or slightly stretch the quilt top to fit the border strips as necessary. Sew the side borders in place with a ¼"-wide seam allowance and press the seam allowances toward the border strips. (I sew with the borders on the bottom to make sure all the seam allowances fall in the intended direction.)

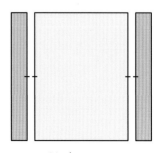

Mark centers.

3. Measure the width of the quilt in three places (include the just-added borders) and determine the average. Cut two strips to this measurement, piecing as necessary. Mark the center of the quilt edges and border strips. Pin the borders to the quilt top, matching the centers and ends, and sew them in place Press the seam allowances toward the border strips.

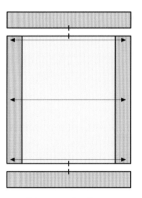

Measure in three places, side to side. Mark centers.

QUILTING

All of the quilts in this book have been quilted on a long-arm quilting machine. Check with the quilter before preparing your finished quilt top and backing to determine the correct size of backing needed, and leave layering to the professional quilter. If you plan to quilt by hand or on your home sewing machine, the quilt top, batting, and backing will need to be layered and basted together before quilting.

BINDING YOUR QUILT

All the bindings for the quilts in this book were cut 2¼" wide across the width of fabric and pieced. I prefer a smaller binding, but if you like a wider binding, cut the strips 2½" wide. Machine baste around the edges about ⅛" from the edge of the quilt top. Trim the batting and backing so that it extends about 1" beyond the edges of the quilt top on all sides.

1. Cut strips as specified in the cutting directions for your quilt
2. To make one long, continuous strip, piece the strips at right angles and stitch across the corner as shown. Trim the excess fabric, leaving a ¼"-wide seam allowance, and press the seam allowances open.

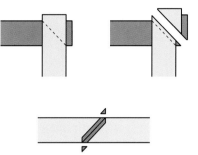

3. Cut one end of the long binding strip at a 45° angle and turn under ¼" as shown. Press the strip in half lengthwise, wrong sides together and raw edges aligned.

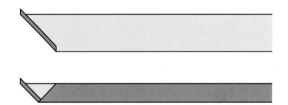

4. Beginning with the angled end of the binding strip, align the raw edge of the strip with the raw edge of the quilt top. Starting on one side (not in a corner) and beginning 3" from the angled end, use a walking foot and a ¼"-wide seam allowance to stitch the binding to the quilt. Stop ¼" from the first corner and backstitch.

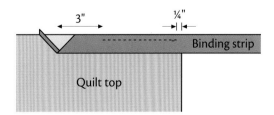

5. Remove the quilt from the sewing machine. Fold the binding straight up and away from the quilt so the fold forms a 45° angle.

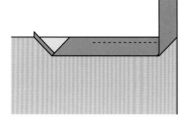

6. Fold the binding back down onto itself, even with the edge of the quilt top, to create an angled pleat at the corner and pin in place. Begin with a backstitch at the fold of the binding and continue stitching along the edge of the quilt top, mitering each corner as you come to it.

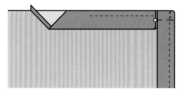

7. Stop stitching approximately 3" from the starting end of the binding strip and backstitch. Remove the quilt from the machine. Trim the binding tail 1" longer than needed and tuck the end inside the beginning of the strip. Pin in place, making sure the strip lies flat. Then finish stitching the binding to the quilt top. Trim the excess batting and backing even with the quilt top.

Trim.

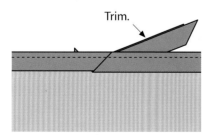

8. Turn the binding to the back of the quilt. Using thread to match the binding, hand stitch the binding in place so that the folded edge covers the row of machine stitching. At each corner, fold the binding to form a miter on the back of the quilt.

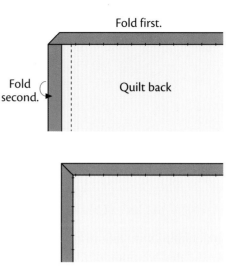

Fold first.

Fold second.

Quilt back

Hanging Sleeve

I make sleeves for all of my quilts immediately after the quilt is complete. From the leftover backing fabric, cut an 8½"-wide strip of fabric equal to the width of the quilt. Because of all the different hangers my quilts hang on in quilt shows or quilt shops, I usually cut a 10½"-wide strip to make a wider sleeve.

1. Fold the short ends over to the wrong side about ½", and then fold ½" again. Press and stitch the folds to create a hem on each end.

2. Fold the strip in half lengthwise, right sides together, and stitch the raw edges together using a ½"-wide seam allowance to make a tube. Press the seam allowances open and turn the tube right side out. Press the sleeve with the seam positioned toward the bottom of the tube and a small fold at the top as shown. (The fold allows space for the rod so the quilt isn't pulled out of shape when hanging.)

Fold →
Seam →

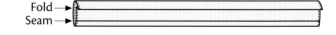

3. Center the sleeve on the back of the quilt, about 1" below the top edge, with the fold and seam line on top, not next to the quilt. Pin in place, and then slip-stitch the top and the bottom edges and both ends of the sleeve to the quilt back, being careful that your stitches do not go through to the front of the quilt.

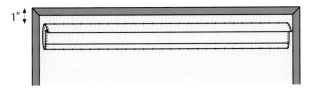

LABEL AND SIGN YOUR QUILT

Future generations will want to know who made your quilt. A label provides important information, including the name of the quilt, who made it, when it was made, and where it was made. You may also want to include the name of the recipient, if it's a gift, and any other interesting or important information about the quilt.

You can stabilize your label fabric by ironing a piece of freezer paper to the wrong side. Use a fine-tipped permanent fabric pen to record the information on the fabric, and then remove the freezer paper. Attach it to the back of the quilt with small stitches. If you have an embroidery machine, you have an added advantage. You can make a beautiful label with all the needed information.

If theft is a concern, you can add the same information to the inside of the sleeve or even behind the sleeve, in addition to the label. No one will look for the second identifying label.

About the Author

Jo Parrott began quilting in 1982 and has made over 500 quilts since that time. She likes to make traditional quilts easier to assemble. The great joys of her life are her 24 grandchildren, her 11 great-grandchildren, and her quilting students. Jo and her husband, Henry, owned a quilt shop in Dallas, Not Just Quilts, for six years and presently live in East Texas in a home they built themselves. When Jo kept stacking up quilt tops that needed to be quilted, Henry decided to try his hand at making a long-arm quilting machine for her. Jo quilted 49 quilts the first year she had it and has now quilted 109 quilts.

New and Best-Selling Titles from

 That Patchwork Place®

America's Best-Loved
Quilt Books®

 *Martingale*®
& COMPANY

America's Best-Loved Craft & Hobby Books®
America's Best-Loved Knitting Books®

APPLIQUÉ
Appliqué Quilt Revival
Beautiful Blooms
Cutting-Garden Quilts
Dream Landscapes
Easy Appliqué Blocks
Simple Comforts
Sunbonnet Sue and Scottie Too

BABIES AND CHILDREN
Baby's First Quilts
Let's Pretend
Snuggle-and-Learn Quilts for Kids
Sweet and Simple Baby Quilts
Warm Welcome—NEW!

BEGINNER
Color for the Terrified Quilter
Four-Patch Frolic—NEW!
Happy Endings, Revised Edition
Machine Appliqué for the Terrified Quilter
Quilting Your Style—NEW!
Your First Quilt Book (or it should be!)

GENERAL QUILTMAKING
American Jane's Quilts for All Seasons
Bits and Pieces
Bold and Beautiful
Country-Fresh Quilts
Creating Your Perfect Quilting Space
Fat-Quarter Quilting—NEW!
Fig Tree Quilts: Fresh Vintage Sewing
Folk-Art Favorites
Follow-the-Line Quilting Designs
    Volume Three
Gathered from the Garden
The New Handmade
Points of View
Prairie Children and Their Quilts
Quilt Challenge—NEW!
Quilt Revival
A Quilter's Diary
Quilter's Happy Hour

Quilting for Joy
Quilts from Paradise—NEW!
Remembering Adelia
Simple Seasons
Skinny Quilts and Table Runners
Twice Quilted

HOLIDAY AND SEASONAL
Candy Cane Lane—NEW!
Christmas Quilts from Hopscotch
Comfort and Joy
Deck the Halls—NEW!
Holiday Wrappings

HOOKED RUGS, NEEDLE FELTING, AND PUNCHNEEDLE
Miniature Punchneedle Embroidery
Needle Felting with Cotton and Wool
Needle-Felting Magic

PAPER PIECING
A Year of Paper Piecing
Easy Reversible Vests, Revised Edition
Paper-Pieced Mini Quilts
Show Me How to Paper Piece

PIECING
501 Rotary-Cut Quilt Blocks
Favorite Traditional Quilts Made Easy
Loose Change
Mosaic Picture Quilts
New Cuts for New Quilts
On-Point Quilts
Ribbon Star Quilts
Rolling Along

QUICK QUILTS
40 Fabulous Quick-Cut Quilts
Charmed, I'm Sure—NEW!
Instant Bargello
Quilts on the Double
Sew Fun, Sew Colorful Quilts
Supersize 'Em!

SCRAP QUILTS
Nickel Quilts
Save the Scraps
Scrap-Basket Surprises
Simple Strategies for Scrap Quilts

CRAFTS
A to Z of Sewing
Art from the Heart
The Beader's Handbook
Dolly Mama Beads
Embellished Memories
Friendship Bracelets All Grown Up
Making Beautiful Jewelry
Paper It!
Trading Card Treasures

KNITTING & CROCHET
365 Crochet Stitches a Year
365 Knitting Stitches a Year
A to Z of Knitting
All about Crochet—NEW!
All about Knitting
Amigurumi World
Amigurumi Two!—NEW!
Beyond Wool
Cable Confidence
Casual, Elegant Knits
Crocheted Pursenalities
Knitted Finger Puppets
The Knitter's Book of Finishing
    Techniques
Knitting Circles around Socks
*Knitting More Circles around
    Socks—NEW!*
Knits from the North Sea—NEW!
More Sensational Knitted Socks
*New Twists on Twined Knitting—
    NEW!*
Pursenalities
Simple Stitches
Toe-Up Techniques for Hand-
    Knit Socks, Revised Edition
Together or Separate

Our books are available at bookstores and your favorite craft, fabric, and yarn retailers. If you don't see the title you're looking for, visit us at **www.martingale-pub.com** or contact us at:

1-800-426-3126
International: 1-425-483-3313
Fax: 1-425-486-7596 • Email: info@martingale-pub.com